One Soul

More Poems
From the Heart
Of Yoga

by
Danna Faulds

Peaceable Kingdom Books
Greenville, Virginia

Additional copies of this book,
and Danna Faulds' first book,
Go In and In are available by mail.
Send $15.00 (includes postage) to:
Danna Faulds
53 Penny Lane
Greenville VA 24440
The author may be reached by e-mail at
yogapoems@aol.com

ISBN 0-9744106-1-6

Printed in the U.S.A. by
Morris Publishing
3212 East Highway 30
Kearney, NE 68847
1-800-650-7888

Dedicated with gratitude to Swami Kripalu, who saw himself as a pilgrim on the path of love and sought to realize the truth that the whole world is one family.

And to everyone, everywhere who aspires to live in that spirit.

Introduction

I am amazed at the gifts I receive simply by taking a little time each day to write. My practice is to make myself available and receptive, to create a bit of space and time, even if it is only five minutes in the morning. When I pick up a pen and begin to write, I open myself to the unknown. I learn a great deal from letting words flow onto the page without editing or judgment, tapping into something within me that is unsullied, whole, and very willing to be revealed. For me, writing serves as a doorway into the mysteries of life and death, separation and oneness, yearning and experience. Words can even create a bridge to divinity, as acknowledged by the powerful opening statement of John's Gospel: "In the beginning was the Word; the Word was with God and the Word was God."

When I delivered the manuscript of my first book *Go In and In* to the printer in the summer of 2002, I thought I had "graduated." In fact, I'd only begun a new chapter in the process of self-discovery that writing is for me. In the last year, I have been deeply touched and humbled by the response of readers. Letters, e-mails and face-to-face conversations have reminded me how alike we all are, how all of us long to awaken and remember truth, how coming into a living relationship with Spirit is nourishing no matter what form it takes.

Writing is not just something that I do, but part of who I am. As I've allowed myself to write with more freedom, I am often surprised by the result. I've written things I didn't know I knew until they appeared before me on the page. I've written poems that have pushed my emotional buttons, caused me to question basic, core assumptions, and ask "Who am I to write, and then to publish these things?" And yet, what could possibly be gained by refusing to share who I am, or withholding the words that come through me? I think the world needs more bridges, not more walls. It is in that spirit of openness and connection that I share these poems.

The poetry in this book falls naturally into two categories. There are "Poems from the Inner Realm," those flowing from experiences in yoga, meditation, prayer or stillness. And there are "Poems from the Outer Realm," inspired by nature, or called forth by external circumstances. Whatever the category, each poem is my attempt to capture and communicate some small part of the journey we all share.

Danna Spitzform Faulds
August, 2003

Acknowledgments

First and always, I thank my husband, Richard Faulds, whose love and support sustains me, and whose editorial assistance was invaluable. I thank Jonathan Foust, President of Kripalu Center, who got me started in the practice of writing, and who lends his prodigious creativity and energy to keep Kripalu Center a vital and evolving sanctuary for Spirit. And I thank Yogi Amrit Desai, who brought Swami Kripalu's teachings to America, and introduced thousands of people to the path of yoga.

To everyone who bought, read, appreciated or shared *Go In and In* with friends or yoga students – this new book wouldn't exist without you. Heartfelt thanks to each of you.

To the participants in the yoga classes and workshops at our home in Greenville, Virginia, at Kripalu Center, and other locations, your openness to transformation inspires me and helps me to keep writing.

To friends and family who have sustained me throughout this journey, offering unique gifts to the rich mix of my life, I'm more grateful than I can say.

Special thanks to: George and Mary Lou Buck, Billy Cape, Stephen Cope, Bettina Dudley, John and Kay Faulds, Aruni Nan Futuronsky, Rupali Cynthia Geesey, Jack Glasser, Ann Greene, Derek Hansen, Martha Harris, Carol Harty, Bill Hydon, Dan Jones, Guy Kettelhack, Margaret and Lloyd Klapperich, Kathy Kuser, Shrila Leslie Luppino, Vandita Kate Marchesiello, Andrea Mather, Audrey McLaughlin, Justin and Adele Morreale, Lawrence Noyes, Navin John Panzer, Deva Parnell, Len and Ling Ming Poliandro, Marc and Meryl Rudin, Bill and Lila Schafer, Hal Spitzform, Marianne Spitzform, Peter Spitzform, Don Thomson, Marc Paul Volavka, Amy Weintraub, and Paul Weiss.

PART I

POEMS FROM

THE INNER REALM

One Soul

When one soul is set ablaze
by truth, the whole universe
ignites, and for an instant
light reaches every corner,
cave and crevasse. When

the heart remembers what
it is, joined in vastness by
joy and suffering, both the
future and the past dissolve
like snowflakes on the tongue.

There is nowhere to run, no
reason to do anything but
rest in the cradle of the
cosmos, rocked in the arms
of emptiness, and held in
the near embrace of love.

Breath By Breath

Life proceeds breath by breath.
Deep, full and easy, shallow or
uneven, breathing is the key to
cultivating peace.

Breath by breath, choose to
stay present. It's isn't success
you are seeking, but surrender
to the flow of energy.

It's not control that matters,
but letting go, allowing life
exactly as it is this moment
to touch and change and
breathe through you.

White Dove

In the shared quiet, an
invitation arises like a
white dove lifting from
a limb and taking flight.

Come and live in truth.
Take your place in the
flow of grace. Draw
aside the veil you thought
would always separate
your heart from love.

All you ever longed for is
before you in this moment
if you dare draw in a
breath and whisper "Yes."

Inexhaustible Supply

There is no distance,
after all, between the
heart and the object
of its longing, no gap
between theory and
experience. It's all
here in easy reach.

This isn't a secret
teaching, locked away
from the uninitiated.
Ask, and All That Is
responds. Knock, and
in some corner, a door
opens. Pray and the
day is different.

Like fruit at harvest
time, love is mine
for the gathering and
giving, always an
inexhaustible supply.

The only proof of
this is in living as
if the source of love
will not run dry. To
fear that I might prime
the pump and find
nothing in my cupped
and waiting hands is to
doubt the One who
authors everything.
Why go there?

Deconstruction

I am deconstructing.
My identity, built
assumption by assumption,
is crumbling at my feet.
It's clear to me the way
of truth leads into the
unknown, but a small, scared
voice inside me cries,
"Not yet. I'm not ready.
Can't you see I need more
preparation?" Balanced
on the rubble, I grope for
handholds even as I try
to let go. I am bared to the
bone by pain and the thwarted
desire to maintain control. I
long to paint the scene the
way I want, while ignoring
how it is. My practice now
isn't about rebuilding what
I knew. It's not about
clearing the littered ground
of old illusions only to
construct new ones.
Emptiness has a stark
beauty, noticed only
when I stop looking
for security. I sit on the
tumble of mortar and brick
and pray for patience,
pray for strength,
pray for the humility
to just keep breathing.

Building Castles

You realize, of course,
    that life has its own
plans. It's fine to go
    forward, draw up
complex schemes,
    watch your dreams
play out as if each
    scene is real. Just be
willing to drop it all
    when truth comes calling.
Let every grain of sand
    fall from your cupped
hands and see the unkempt
    pile on the ground equally
as valuable as that castle
    you were building.
Allow the tide to scour all
    of it away, every trace,
and replace it with the
    sea's own beauty.

Self-Observation Without Judgment

Release the harsh and pointed inner
voice. It's just a throwback to the past,
and holds no truth about this moment.

Let go of self-judgment, the old,
learned ways of beating yourself up
for each imagined inadequacy.

Allow the dialogue within the mind
to grow friendlier, and quiet. Shift
out of inner criticism and life
suddenly looks very different.

I can say this only because I make
the choice a hundred times a day
to release the voice that refuses to
acknowledge the real me.

What's needed here isn't more
prodding toward perfection, but
intimacy – seeing clearly, and
embracing what I see.

Love, not judgment, sows the
seeds of tranquility and change.

Posture Flow

This is a sacrament,
a prayer of breath, a
symphony of soul
and motion. This is
yoga, emerging from
the inside, out – all
here in this singular
meditation of spirit.
Trust that the body
knows what it needs
if you dare to follow
where it leads.

The Practice of
Being Present

Attend the breath.
Let the rhythm
slow and settle.
Filling, emptying,
draw the outside
in, and then release.
Simplicity and ease.
Nothing to do but
breathe, relax and
feel the free
movement of air
and life force,
watch the play
of energy and
sensation, allow
everything to be,
without the need
to change or fix or
make it different.
This moment, you
can listen to your
soul. This breath,
you can have no
goal but being. You
are already complete.
This, just this, is
what it means
to be whole.

Deeper Practice

The call to deeper practice comes,
and I respond before I catch myself.
All that I am is drawn inside as if
pulled by the strongest tide, a current
flowing in only one direction.

What does this practice look like?
Slow movement paired with breath,
attunement, trust, surrender. I
listen within. Called forward,
I let go into the unknown.

Thy will be done, Lord, but at this
depth, I cannot see the difference
between my will and Yours. There
is only breath, the sound of one word,
"Yes," repeating with each heartbeat.

Yes, I still have an individual identity.
Yes there are still thoughts and preferences,
yet these pale to insignificance before the
door I've opened. I step inside the realm
of Spirit and let myself be changed.

Intimate With All Things

The Buddha said, "I am
intimate with all things."
Imagine that. To be on
the same close terms with
suffering and panic as bliss
and rapture; to know the
souls of water buffalo as
surely as my own; to push
away nothing; to let the
sweet or bitter taste of
life linger; to see the
Beloved in everything –
and when that isn't my
experience, to be intimate
with self-hatred, unmet
preferences and the many
ways I don't show up as
saintly. Imagine that.

Metaphor

Lying on the floor, in
the middle of a yoga pose,
I stretch my left arm out
as far as it extends,

and see my fingers slip
inside a square of light
the sun casts on the carpet.

For a moment, I know
myself as metaphor, the
seeker always reaching for
more, the mythic journey

out of night, longing for
the luminous. I fill my
lungs with breath, find

the apex of the stretch,
watch a wave of feeling
crest, and flow into the

next pose, my warm left
hand carrying the sun's
message into shadow.

The Doubt du Jour

He enters surely as if I'd
issued him a key, sits on
the most comfortable couch
and starts to order me around.
"You," he says, pointing a
bony finger in the direction
of my head. (My doubts are
never feminine.) He sounds
like he grew up in Brooklyn.
"Who the hell do you think
you are?" A skeptical leer
twists his lips as he says this.
"You think you can pen a line
or two and call yourself a poet?
You think you can trust the
universe to provide for you
outside the normal nine to
five? That's sheer and utter
bullshit." (I've noticed if I'm
not cowering by this point,
the figure on the couch
expands, the pointing finger,
a sausage, out of all proportion,
tries to pin me down). "You
good for nothing, worthless
scum, you selfish, lazy,
dysfunctional excuse of a
woman." Here's where
it gets really interesting.
If I can let the voice of Doubt
just be there, without controlling
me, it starts to fade. He sounds
like the Wicked Witch after
Dorothy pitched water at her face.

The accusations wane. But if I
attempt to defend myself the
battle lines are drawn. Doubt
calls in reinforcements. He
mimics my mother's voice
with uncanny artistry. He
dredges in the mud for scenes
from my past and puts them on
parade. He grows so wide and
loud he drowns out the birds,
the sound of rain on window
panes, the music of the wind.
This is where practice comes
in handy, when being fifty
is far easier than twenty-five.
So Doubt stands up and almost
fills the room. He lists my
imperfections one by one
until I feel like a beetle in
some kid's bug collection with
a pin through my middle, and
I'm praying for the chloroform.
But here's the thing. If I can
get a little distance from the
drama of it all, if I can witness
this instead of playing dead,
if I can laugh at Doubt, he
simply disappears. Oh yeah,
he'll be back. He's waiting
in the wings. But even one
good belly laugh will banish
him again. That's the way
it is with me and Doubt.

Being Home

Where can I soften
in this posture?
Where is the edge
between opening
and force, the line
between stretch and
too much effort?

The mind and body
serve up a feast of
feelings, each breath
another chance to
deepen and release.

The smallest motion,
or even just a quiet
sigh could be all that
I require to shift my
focus from the outer
to the inner realm,
a change from feeling
lost to being home.

Meditation on the Mind

I sit on the cushion and watch
    my thoughts. How strange, this
world that I concoct, full of
    worry, danger, details and
possible scenarios that never
    actually play out. The mind
is engineered for this, for
    solving problems, listing differences,
casting about for things to fix.
    Though it can bind me as effectively
as rope and leg irons,
    I couldn't do without it.

And yet, there's also this. Within,
    behind, or deeper than the surface mind
there's something vast and unified,
    where first and last are not opposites,
but equal partners on a path so
    paradoxical it can't be tamed or grasped.

There is peace so unmoving
    it embraces both reality and pain.
There is the stark truth that
    nothing on the mind's to-do
list is important enough to lose
    touch with what's essential.

Peace and problem-solving
    are not mutually exclusive.
It's up to me to recognize
    the potential for judging
neither as wrong or
    right. After all, the whole
spectrum is contained in a
    single ray of natural light.

Let Go of Something

Let go of something,
somewhere. Use yoga
to become aware, to
touch what lies beneath
the surface of the skin.
Is there tension longing
for release; a knot of
fear so deep and familiar
that you believe it's
part of who you are?

Ease into dark corners,
locked rooms, unexplored
hallways. Gain entry
not by force or will
but only by softness.
Enter on the wings of
breath, and turn the
key of self-acceptance
to let go of something,
somewhere.

Desire

Buddhists say desire is a
hindrance, but I see it as
an invitation. It opens
doors, draws me outside
my smaller self, inspires
me to be creative. Desire
is the proof that I'm alive.

The lesson lies in whether
I can value emptiness as
much as being filled. If I
can live with wants and let
them go, if I can know that
I don't know, then desire
is one among the many
paths to freedom.

Another Meditation Poem

I try to meditate,
and my mind races
like a rodent through
a maze. It's got no
place to hide, no
corner for retreat. It
doesn't like to face
itself head on.
Instead of focusing
on technique, my
mind begins to
write a poem. I
repeat a Sanskrit
chant, but that gets
lost in a whirl of
unrelated thought.
I concoct a vivid
soap opera in my
head, then lose track
of the story's thread,
and redesign the
bedroom. My senses
search for anything
alluring – the sound
of wind, the far off
raucous call of crows,
the feel of blankets on
my knees. Just when
I'm convinced it's
time to trudge off in
defeat, there is a
momentary opening,
a second of pure
stillness. Thoughts

rush back in, but I
know then there's
a reason to persist
in sitting. Something
slowly shifts. Now,
mind you, this lasts
only for the briefest
instant, but I know
myself as whole. No
fireworks, no drama,
no territory gained,
just a breath or two
when all that isn't
true falls away and
the spaciousness that
remains stuns the
mind to silence. This
is why I choose to sit.
It's not about a distant
victory. No, meditating
is here and now, a very
present glimpse of all
that is, a chance
to just be whole.

Gather me into your wide
embrace.

My heart races, sings, shouts,
drums out its chorus of desire.

Sweep me off my feet.
I will not protest.

Transport me to the only
source of poems and
stillness.

When I arrive at your
inner chamber, the craving
is like fire.

Remove from me the
finery of my illusions
until I am stripped bare,
awareness so focused
that I know the very

moment we shift from
two to one, from
expectation to lovemaking,
from longing into bliss.

I can put no words to this,
but I am all here, no inch
of me untouched, awake
in a way that defies
definition,

taking you in, giving up
        everything and nothing,
        so unbearably whole
that I forget I was
        ever separate.

I know you will not remind me.

One With Truth

When I recognize that
I am one with truth and
the whole searing, seamless
universe, I don't need proof.
I stop seeking reassurance.

This knowing is too strong
to second-guess or push
away – it's what I am.
It seeps in, leaks out,
changes everything and
leaves me much the same.

It isn't a realization, really –
more an experience of what
has always been, and will be.
There are no separate pieces
in this creation – not one of
us exists outside the whole.

Lineage Holders

What does it mean to hold the teachings
of past masters? Links in a chain that
stretches back in time, we walk the fine
line between honoring what came before
and birthing a new vision as vast as the
dance of the deities.

What keeps a lineage vibrant, enlivens
practices with the energy of truth and
transformation? What weaves individual
souls into the whole cloth of tradition,
and a great work moving forward
through the ages?

It is remembrance and the willingness
to let go of form. It is bold dreams
and fearless action. It is taking the
teachings into the fray of everyday
life, saying yes to what the moment
holds. It is intractable chaos and
creative commitment. It is blazing
a trail, bushwhacking in the dark
without a flashlight. It is riding
a wave of truth with the power
to change the landscape and the
lives of all it touches.

Whether we chose the path or it
chose us, we can shake the dust
from our feet and walk forward
without looking back – each step
a part of the lineage unfolding.

Beneath the Surface

What will I know if I go
below the choppy surface
of the mind? Focus flows,
and there are no fixed points.
Slow currents swirl, and slip
still deeper. I grow very quiet.
The mind attends the subtlest
sensations. It is a different
world and I am an explorer
of these inner realms, where
nothing stays the same for
very long. Energy shifts and
changes. I find peace beneath
the surface, bring it back with
me, hold it in my hands like a
small, white bird and then
release it, that peace might
fly where it's most needed.

Everything I Think I'm Missing

I am struggling. There's who I
believe I ought to be, and who
I really am. It's humbling, isn't
it? This being, this mystery, this
me sits here radiating energy, yet
I'm gripped by a nameless fear
that I'm missing exactly what
I came to experience.

I am suffering, telling myself
stories of what life should look
like. And then I get the message
like a meteor, like the power
coming back on after hours
in a storm.

This life, this extraordinary
imperfection, this moment
just as it is, this is all I'm
here to receive. The infuriating,
limitless simplicity of day-to-
day living holds everything
I think I'm missing.

In the Depths

Mine is a mind
entirely out of synch
with divine reality –
today at least it is.

Biochemically challenged
synapses fire, but the
dire visions they spew
forth do not inspire
anything but shrinking
in despair.

If I took this inner
dialogue as truth –
and it all feels so
very real – I would
never dare to
write another word,
or do anything of
consequence again.

Choosing not to
be deceived –
making the decision
to believe I'm
more than these
bleak thoughts,
takes every ounce
of energy and
every bit of
faith I've got.

Love Laughs

Listen. Love laughs
at fear. Can you hear it?
And fear fades in the face
of laughter. Let nothing
distract you from the fact
that fear will grow if you
feed it, and shrink when
you pay it no heed. There.
See? Fear disappears, and
leaves love laughing.

Infinite Embrace

I will hold you, rock you,
shake you awake, take you
in my arms and speak the
secrets of creation. Oh, do
not push me away, even if
your doubts say that such
intimacy as this is saved
only for the holy or the
realized, those perfect ones
whose feet don't ever touch
the ground. I tell you that
grace falls equally among
all sentient creatures. You
that see me, know me, taste
the sweetness of my skin
against your cheek, it is
your awareness through
which I live and breathe
and have my being. It is
your love that lends me
form and weight, your
willingness to be in truth
that gives our union shape.
It is your choice, you saying
"Yes!" again and again that
allows our infinite embrace.

Flowing Focus

Absorption, the flow
of focus riding on
the breath. Intent,
senses riveted on
the sound and feel
of spirit, on breath
drawn in and then
released.

This is how the Holy
One is received –
communion of air and
energy, the slow reach
of limbs and stretch of
torso – the body as
a doorway in.

Goddess of the Night

The goddess of the night
spoke only in a quiet
voice. "Trust the movement
of energy," she said. "Trust
the opening of blossoms.
Trust the wisdom that
rises through you like sap
flows through trees in
spring. Trust the leave-
taking of that which you
don't need, and the coming
of new insight."

The goddess pushed the
cloud-hair from her eyes
and offered me a cup.
"This is the chalice of
life, the chalice of
change and choice.
Drink deeply," she said,
and do not second-guess
yourself. The only answers
worth listening to are those
that come from deep within."

With the approach of dawn,
the goddess transformed
herself in sunrise. As the
last stars faded in the sky,
she spoke to me a final time:
"Trust your own immortal
soul. Trust what you know
and what you don't. Trust

that you can do what's yours
to do. Trust life to bring you
face to face with truth.

How? The question is a
    dead end, a solid wall, no
doors or windows. How?
    If I insist on knowing
everything before I begin,
    I might as well give up now.
How to do what's mine to do?
    Often I start off without a clue.
I take one step and the next one
    just comes clear. Or maybe I'm
left standing for a time, unsure
    which foot to move, what fork
in the road to choose. This can
    feel like dying, twisting slowly
in the wind. Then when I least
    expect it, I get exactly what I
need. I won't let "how" hold
    me captive any more. How to
write a poem? How to know
    God? How to be loving or
compassionate? I've tasted all
    these gifts, but still can't tell
you how I did it. The instruction
    guide for life comes only in
installments. How to do a
    particular task isn't always
listed in the index, but I'll tell
    you my experience . There's
a sure link between faith and
    finding out. The cosmos works
through flow, not certainty. The
    mind still wants the question
answered beyond doubt, but the
    soul sees its freedom in not
needing to know how.

Light Pours Into Light

I sit on the cushion
using will, applying
firm determination to
stay still. It is an ordinary
morning, thoughts and
stories flitting through
the mind like Spring
birds at the feeder –
going, coming, singing,
fighting. My mind is
anything but quiet. And
then there is a shift.

Light pours into light,
and the small being
that was me expands.
There is open space
and energy, as if the
cosmos chose to birth
itself within my breast.

Light pours into light,
and then I'm back in
ordinary time and thought,
birds begging me for
more seed in the feeder.

Circle

When we sit here in a
circle and grow still,
the energy of Spirit
fills us. Until we
surrender to silence,
we stay on the choppy
surface of the mind.
As the breath grows
quiet, we go behind
thought, beneath
confusion, fear and
doubt. When we sit
here in a circle and
grow still, the mystery
of truth and vastness
transforms our separate
energies into one heart,
one consciousness,
one being – present
and fulfilled.

Precisely Where You Are

There is no turning back, you
    know. Once the soul is awake,
and the voice of spirit beckons,
    there is only one direction. Of
course, the route may look a
    bit circuitous. Yes, it may
look as if you move every which
    way but forward until you see
the broader view, the one that
    shows you with arms thrown
wide, embracing absolutely
    everything, your long stride
carrying you to the exact spot
    on which you stand.

The path to truth moves through
    some quite peculiar landscapes,
and there are times you'll swear
    you're going nowhere.
But if you tried to iron out
    the twists and turns and make it
all into a perfect, straight and
    narrow walk to the finish line –
think how boring and predictable
    that would be! Where you need
to be right now is here, just here,
    precisely where you are.

Center of the Stream

Soften. Soften. Sink into
the still center and receive
the body's wisdom. Drink
it in. Feel everything. (Can
I really risk embodiment?)

Breathe until sensations rise
in a wave. The feelings I've
always pushed away now
take center stage. (Am I
strong enough to witness this?)

Relax. A deep, connected
breath sends the message,
"All is well," even as
sensations swell. (Can I drop
the masks and feel the armor
start to crack?)

A parade of stories, needs
and dreams move past. (Can
I watch them all and not react?)

This moment is unfolding,
whole, unique, felt and seen.
(Dare I allow myself to be
carried to the center of the
stream where the water is
too deep to stand, and
there are no handholds?)

Swallowed Whole

When I let go of what I
know, what's left? If I
set off without a compass,
will I be led? An inner urge
too strong to overlook insists
that I go forward. I stumble,
fall, get up and start again.
Longing lights the path like
a lantern. The mountaintop
looks so far away that I
stop to rest, and in the quiet
I realize that practice isn't
about getting anywhere,
changing anything, making
something happen or slowing
what's in motion. Union
can't be forced, won't be won
by fighting. It alights like a
moth on a dandelion or swallows
me whole like Jonah's whale.
All it takes is receiving what
is here right now, being intimate
with all that is, and knowing that
the act of offering what I really
am will never be refused.

For Anyone Who's Ever Felt Unloved

It was a long and
arduous fast, a time
of short rations, but
now it's past. Feed
your heart love
sandwiches. Serve
tea from a silver
pot with the word
"Beloved" etched
in a fine and steady
hand. Let peach
juice drip down
your chin, each
kiss of fuzzy skin
to lip a reminder
of sweetness.
Sniff the bowl of
wild roses, each
blossom wide
open as if to
tender you the
fullest expression
of affection, as if
to say, "You are
the most cherished
being in the world
today."

Follow Truth

The Buddha didn't know that
his choice to be himself would
roll through the pages of history
like a rogue wave. All he did

was sit beneath the bodhi tree,
intention fixed on awakening,
and when the light flowed in,
he offered it back as the fruit

of all his practice. We each
act without knowing how the
ripples from our pond might
touch another, what the

consequences of our freedom
might be, or where the choice
to follow truth might lead.

You Know Me

We are intimately acquainted, you and me.

I am the Creator and Sustainer, the life force
that animates the trees, the faith that transforms
belief into something deeper.

I am as eloquent in death as birth, the always and
forever essence of emptiness and breath.

Speak any of ten thousand names and I am there
before the words leave your lips.

It is I who lift the heavens up, bind water into ice
or send it flowing toward the ocean.

You know me in every moment, yet you can't own,
define, or even make me line up with what your mind
would posit as reality.

My presence doesn't leave when your awareness
shifts from prayer to serving tea. The mind will
often need to focus elsewhere, but that doesn't
change the truth of me.

There are countless ways I can present myself to you,
but what is it that I truly wish to say?

It's this: Don't miss me in the rush to get things done.
I'm here right now, the pinnacle and root of love.

You don't have to stop doing what is yours to do,
retire to a cave, close the curtains tight, or meditate
from dusk to daylight.

I'm here right now. You are so much a part of me that you tend to miss the forest in the trees.

Choose to behold me. Choose to know me. Choose to acknowledge the communion occurring even as you read these words.

Choice is all that is required for the spark of me within you to catch fire.

Catch a Glimpse of Truth

If I turn at the right moment, I
might catch a glimpse of truth.
In hot pursuit of the ineffable I
could tumble into wonderland,
or lose my footing by sheer chance
and find my whole life changed.

Perfection exists but I can't earn
or grasp it. To walk the edge of
will and surrender, ease and effort,
hope and openness is the only
way to move beyond the
sealed envelope of suffering.

Here's the amazing thing –
the bursting, uncontrolled buoyancy
of Spirit is never content to remain
contained for long. It slips past
my best defenses, and suddenly

I'm outside the known, as if the
looking glass cracked before I
can claim the image mirrored
in the frame. When I sense the
light that shines within, when

energy emanates like a spring
that won't run dry, when I am
revealed to myself for what I
really am, what can I do but raise
my eyes skyward? Thanks be to

the radiance of Spirit, truth tasted,
felt and seen. Thanks be to
everything that came before and
opened a score of doorways
in a life that once held only walls.

I Am Already

One flow of
energy and breath
connects the full
depth and breadth
of consciousness.
There is nowhere to
go but here, no time
but now, no why or
how or maybe – just
the knowing, simple
and complete, that I
am already what I
thought I had to seek.

Choosing Life

The downward spiral starts.
Self-doubt and darkness
vie for center stage, while
I, the passive, drowning
one, wait for my demise.

Just as I sink beneath the
wave of my despair a
thought arises. Why go
there? I've made this
trip a thousand times,
and it leads nowhere.

I'm choosing life. The
darkness lifts just a little.
I'm choosing life. The
downward spiral slows,
then stops. I'm lifted up
and buoyant now, not
shrinking from the truth.

Okay, I'm not perfect,
and reality certainly
doesn't look like
what I'd choose. And
maybe that's the only
point – to ride the spirals
down and up, and make
the choice for life.

Two Myths Take a Hike

Atlas is always shouldering his load.
You know that feeling – the weight
of everything pressing in, suffocating.

And there is Sisyphus pushing the
boulder uphill, over and over. Two
poster boys for ceaseless effort.

But what if (now here's a radical idea,)
the way of transformation is not a
long or tortured change?

What if it's just being here, this moment,
now, complete and whole? What if you
could whisper in Atlas's big ear, "It's
time to let go. Really. The heavens will
not disappear if you put your burden down."

Imagine him thinking about it. Imagine
him believing. See him set the load down,
straighten up, stretch, smile, stride over to
Sisyphus and say something you can't hear.

See the stone roll down, and Sisyphus
choose not to follow. You are the witness
to the shouts of joy, the head shaking
wonder and relief – you mean it's this easy?

Imagine the spring in their step, the lightness
of their laughter as they climb that hill and
disappear from view.

The Operative Conjunction

Every day, a choice to be
made, a thousand decisions
between the dim and fearful
view (I can't do this. I've
bitten off far more than I
can chew) and the other
side (somehow this will
all work out).

The mind insists on
choosing sides, pitting
pessimism against optimism,
not content to let life be
exactly as it is. I imagine
the best or worst, and react
to mere possibility, not
present fact. But the desire
to control and judge, to pick
one experience over another –
is that just what humans do?

Every ingredient is welcome
at life's banquet. There's
nothing wrong with this stew
I'm cooking up. Whatever's
here; the bland or spicy mix
of shadow and light, the
grasping and the pushing back –
it's all equally sacred in the
eyes of the creator. The only
operative conjunction is
"and," not "but." How much

can I let in – both sides and
the middle, front and back,
the water and the wine glass
each are full. The feast of
life is laid out for the tasting.

Buoyant

I am buoyant,
lifted by breath
and the touch
of air on skin.
I am weightless,
borne higher
with each
inhalation, no
ballast or tether;
rising, molecules
mingling with
the scent of
spring. Soaring,
freedom refusing
to be reined in.
I look down on a
cloud of dogwood
flowers and hear
the soft exhalation
of trees. Grass, ants,
earth, atmosphere,
universe, we are all
one being, breathing,
and expanding.
I make the choice to
stay awake, to see,
and let myself be
seen. I hear and
breathe, and fly
and be, and know
that I am known.

Mining Diamonds

I used to be convinced
that if I could shrink
myself smaller than
a pin, smaller than a
mustard seed or comma,

if I could crawl inside
my head like a microbic
coal miner, the canary
would be dead within a
minute. Doesn't it feel

like that? Shine a flash-
light on this mess, and I'll
find out just how slimy,
worthless, and fundamentally
mistaken I really am.

But just the opposite is true.
The more illumination I
bring in, the more I see, the
more caved-in passageways
I excavate –

The more the canary sings
in ecstasy. And the
miner, light reflecting on
wide veins of diamonds –

the miner just stumbled
into paradise.

The Real Deal

There's something in me
that won't give up, that
struggles to stay open and
not just shrug or go numb.
Lord knows, there are a
raft of reasons to pull the
covers over my head,
refuse to get out of bed,
worship at the shrine of
cynical despair. Call it
what you will – the still,
small voice, the light
within, Spirit, life force,
All That Is – no name,
every name, the outcome
is the same. There's
something in me that
just won't roll over and
play dead despite the tall
odds stacked against it.
I mean, if we were playing
Charades, what could I say?
"Sounds like – pain."
"Sounds like – First you
struggle, then you die."
I can't dispute the truth
that life is hard, and certainly
not smooth. And yet, and
still, and once again, I try.
I reach inside and find a
moment of wonder, the
urge to love, the truth that
we're all walking in the
same direction. If I can

write a poem, cook a meal,
plant a few seeds, if I can leave
the world a better place today
for having lived, isn't that
enough? Yeah, I know. I
want proof too, or lacking
that, at least a dramatic
scene where I'm swept
away by a tidal wave of
bliss, never to suffer again.
The real deal is the choice
to stay awake in the face
of what is actually happening.
It's the unbearable truth that
I and you and all of us are
learning to be human at the
same time that we're divine.
Perfect imperfection. Trial
and error. The universe's
grand experiment. Each one
of us is no less important to
the cosmos than the Big Bang.
I've got my role to play even
if I can't articulate exactly
what it is. All I can do is
say yes to what is mine to
do. Say yes and take a single
step, casting my vote for life
and not a living death.

Breath of God

I feel the Great One breathe me in.
It is a long, deep breath that
stretches me thin, lengthens
me from crown to feet. It
pulls me forward, drawing me
through the impossibly small
eye of a needle I can barely
see. And then I'm on the
other side, where God's heart
is beating. Am I inside the
heart of God, or is it God who
moves in me? Pierced through
with the thread of love, I neither
know, nor care. I feel the
Great One breathe me out, feel
the wind at my back, and I am
sailing, flying, crying out,
weeping with joy and sadness.
Then I breathe God in, one long,
deep breath, reaching from here
to the soul of the infinite.

Joy For No Reason

I am filled with quiet
joy for no reason save
the fact that I'm alive.
The message I receive
is clear – there's no time
to lose from loving, no
place but here to offer
kindness, no day but this
to be my true, unfettered
self and pass the flame
from heart to heart. This
is the only moment that
exists – so simple, so
exquisite, and so real.

A Simple Conversation

"I'm listening, God,"
says I, in the middle of
a sleepless night. "Me
too," came the immediate
reply. I knew this to be
true from the pregnant
void so patiently awaiting
my next move. So I
thought awhile before
I said, "I just want to
see you…" When I
pause, the reply comes
sure and short: "That's
what I want too – to see
every unedited, unabashed,
passionate, playful, creative,
crazy, naked inch of you."

Now, I had to stop and
take that in, but there was
such unmistakable receptivity
I dared continue. "Well, what
I really mean is I want to know
you – in the biblical sense,
with every cell and pore, in
core and essence." I paused
to take a breath and think
what should come next,
and here is what I heard,
I swear it, word for word.

"Done," God said. "What
you ask for in your heart
of hearts is already true.

We have always been one
being, but the human mind
can't conceive of unity, can't
see the colors of a rainbow as
one undivided whole, insists
on praying to me as if I am
a separate entity. But I tell
you this in perfect truth,
the union you desire is as
close as flame to fire, near
as starlight on the clearest
night. You and I are one.

My kingdom is within you
now, not when you die,
not just if you play all
your cards right, not only
when you strive for perfection,
or failing that, flail yourself
into unholy submission. The
church got that exactly wrong.
It's your humanness, the raw,
imperfect, messy, truth of
you that enables you to know
communion. Stop trying so
hard, and just be you – all
the rest comes as naturally
as this conversation you
are having with yourself."

There was silence as my
pen caught up, then hung
there in mid air. "I love
nothing more than when
you step lightly through
your life, when you laugh

easily and often, and don't
take anything too seriously.
You see, the outcome is
assured. You don't have to
impress, improve, justify or
move heaven and earth to
get my attention. Ask and
I will answer. Look and you
will see. Breathe, and in the
pause between two breaths
you'll find me. Your
language insists on "you"
and "me," but that's not
the way it is. It's "we,"
not separate entities, but
one being, ever changing,
always present, never born
and truly deathless. Amen."
That's every word I heard.
And then I went on back
to bed and slept.

Celebrate the Journey

Who knows why life unfolds
the way it does; why we choose
one path or another, share the
way for a while or a day, then
say goodbye. There is no
predictability here, and less
control than we might wish.
But there is the quiet urging
of the heart, the knowing in
the soul, the wisdom that's
beneath the mind, accessible
if we breathe and turn inside.

When the tide of change rolls
in we can resist or be at peace,
struggle or release. The stuff
of life may not be ours to
understand. It's enough to
offer love, to receive the best
and worst, to embrace and
say farewell. What matters
most is to celebrate each
moment of the journey.

Here

It's always here, the silent
underpinning, the foundation
beneath the foundation. When
I reach deep enough into darkness,

inside fear, self-doubt, aversion or
despair, there's something so intact
I almost miss it in my focus on
brokenness. It's always here, this

ground of being. Like the water in
which fish swim, it's easy to overlook
the eloquence of truth. It's here, this
guiding presence, this calm, abiding

stillness. It's here when I don't try
to make life any more or less than
what it is, when I stop trying to be
right. It's here when I unclench my

fists and breathe, when I let go of the
demand to make life smooth or easy.
It's here, the oneness underlying
multiplicity, the exquisite "is-ness"

of everything. I could shout it from
the rooftops, but it's true no matter
what I say, and I know you'll find
it in your own time, your own way,

that precious moment when you
choose to meet life exactly as it is.

Drinking Wine With Rumi

I sit quietly enough. I really do try,
but inside, I'm chafing at the bit. I
put in my half-hour on the cushion,
but that's it – a night of pent up

energy is itching to express. It's
music that I'm longing for – and
dance. I want to move so freely
that I forget everything else, even

where the walls are, even where
my arms are, even that there is a
world beyond this turning center.
It's dance that makes me happiest,

the unbridled, unedited confluence
of joy and breath, doing anything
and everything that calls for
movement and expression. I take

up space and don't apologize. I
merge with music and lose myself
in movement. There is a reason
Rumi taught the dervishes to whirl.

I meet them all on the dance floor,
drunk and wild-haired, those twelfth
century apostles of poetry and prayer.
They welcome me into the group

as if I've always been there, hand me
a musky, goat skin wine bag and
bid me drink. All that matters is
the energy that courses through

and turns the room into a cathedral.
Rumi and I whirl until the Beloved's
curls are tangled in our own and the
wine skins all lie empty on the floor.

Such a God-intoxicated bunch
I've never seen; Rumi,
the dervishes, and me.

Light Bearers

We are light bearers, stewards
of a truth that insists on being
shared despite doubt or fear or
imagined limitation. We spread
the flame by teaching or by growing
still, by daring to be outrageous
and dancing beneath the full moon,
or by holding a friend in need
and taking part in life's normal
routines. This is our message -
there is hope encoded in each
cell, each loving thought, each
time we reach out to one another.
There's truth that won't be stopped
by toppling buildings, snipers'
bullets, war clouds on the horizon,
or the inner storms of grief, despair
and insecurity. We are the peace we've
been seeking, the peace that stretches
beyond the mind's need for form or
understanding, the peace for which
each human heart longs. Now is
the time for the light bearers to
offer up the truth of who
and what we really are.

PART II

POEMS FROM

THE OUTER REALM

Green

It is a green world,
lush and damp, drops
of water poised on
grass blades, some
leaves large as dinner
plates. To describe
the scene, I need more
words for green. There
must be tropical tongues,
words sprouting from
the depths of rain
forests, languages rich
with more verdant
imagery than English.
It is a green world,
chartreuse, jade,
and olive mix in
the vista like
tossed salad;
cucumber, emerald,
lime, the deep
satisfying green
of pea vines,
the blue-green
of pines in shadow,
the pale green of
early apples
favored by the
deer. Green was
the first thought
I had this morning
when I opened my
eyes, and looked
outside.

Before the Deluge

How did Noah ever choose the
two chinchillas to save from
the deluge, the two gorillas?
Did each species call a caucus,
a solemn gathering of ground-
sloths? Was there a meeting
of weasels, long bodies squeezed
into a clearing in the woods?
Young weasel bucks casting
furtive glances to gauge the
competition, a pair of weasel
parents pushing their comely
daughter through the crowd.
"Take her, she's perfect for
breeding. See how the auburn
fur lays along the hollow of her
back?" Weasel elders try to say
something wise and inspiring,
but they can all hear the sound
of hammers pounding pegs into
that big boat Noah's building
with his sons. Each thud drives
the message deeper. Choose.
Choose soon. Only two of you.
Did a herd of zebras watch the
two they voted "Most Likely
To Succeed In Passing On the
Gene Pool?" Did they wait in
a shuffling clump as hooves hit
the rough hewn wood, watch as
the two anointed ones crossed
that bridge between the doomed
and hope? Did they wave as
rumps and tails disappeared

through the wide door, one last
glint of white before those two
were swallowed by the shadows?
Did the zebras keep waving, or
simply turn away, ears cocked
at the distant, low
rumbling of thunder?

Alfalfa Sprout

I am so ready. Squeezed
inside this tiny seed, I am
coiled energy, waiting for
water and light, waiting to
breathe, waiting for the
green of me to come forth.
Compact potential, waiting
to unwind, waiting to find
my way out, waiting for a
rebirth into something far
different than I've been.
It's time. I know it's time.
Oh, have you ever seen
anything as lovely as this
shoot, this root reaching
out and down, drinking
life in? To create a leaf
worthy of being eaten is a
full-blown miracle to me.

Full Moon

The moon leaned her full,
round face so close to mine
that her mountains touched
the furrows of my brow.

"I have a secret," she said
with a wink. I waited.
"You're not dead until you're
dead," she said. I was a bit
incredulous.

"You're not impressed?" the
moon asked, looking just a
bit perplexed. "Well, let me
put it this way then.

"You've got every single day that
you're alive to really live. Isn't
that due cause for celebration?"
Her enthusiasm was infectious.

The moon bent low, just missing
a collision with a flying wedge of
geese. "So what are you doing
this evening?" she asked. "I'm

being me," I said. "Oh, that's
the best!" the moon replied, and
smiling widely, resumed her
place in the starlit sky.

Black Snake

One afternoon, while
        following an urge to
                walk the lane, I came
                        upon a black snake,
                alive, but motionless
        as stone – no flick of
tongue or blink of eye,
        no smooth slithering
                of skin on grass, no
                        turn of head. I watched,
                my eyes tracing graceful
        curves from nose to tail,
drawn into stillness and
        waiting, compact strength,
                profound patience. I
                        stood, mesmerized for
                a time, then reached out
        my right hand and stroked
slowly down the long,
        black back, once, and
                then again, petting it
                        like a friend. It didn't
                        stir until I said, "I'm afraid
                to leave you here with
your head half on the
        lane where a car could
                put an end to your
                        contemplation." I moved
                my foot, and like black
        lightning, the snake
turned around to look
        at me, then disappeared
                into the woods, a faint
                        movement of grass the

77

only sign I had of its
direction. My fingers
still held the cool
impression of its skin as
I took a step backward.
"Thank you," I said into
the rustling leaves on my
left, and continued
on my way.

Turkey Vultures

A flock of turkey vultures
launches from the pines.
The big birds struggle in
the wind, caught by cross
currents, rising precipitously,
dipping, swerving hard left,
then left again to miss two
trees. One swoops low,
past the window where I
sit, wings cocked just so,
feathers taut and straining.
Its black eyes measure the
distance to the house, revel
in the uncontrollable rush
and sheer of wind. Then it
veers off, lifted by an updraft,
its bald red head like a mark
of punctuation in the sky.

Dancing With the Wind

There is wind so strong
it blows song lyrics
composed in New Orleans
up the valleys to the
Blue Ridge. Trees sway
like women singing the
blues, like grandmothers
rocking sick children,
like the center of the
universe is rhythm, not
a fixed point. There is
wind so fierce it clears
out anything that doesn't
belong here and leaves me
clean as newly written
notes played for the first
time on a silver flute. The
melody tickles my feet
until I dance like the trees,
and gulp great gusts of air.
I stop to rest only after I'm
spent, drunk on the energy
of the evening, hair so
tangled with wind knots
that I play the part of the
wild woman, empress of
the sky, a gypsy sent to
tell the world's fortune and
weave magic into dreams.
The wind blows straight to
the heart of the unknown,
and without a pause,
I follow it home.

Good Morning

Good morning world. I'm
stiff, but optimistic. Good
morning birds. They fly
around the feeder like seed-
seeking missiles. Good
morning breath. I feel the
rise and fall of chest, the
easy out and in that signals
relaxation. Good morning
mist. The low clouds shroud
the mountains, drift through
the yard like wisps of smoke.
Good morning heart. Its
slow rhythm keeps me
company. The day awoke
two hours ago, and I'm just
catching up. Senses take in
this morning like a sponge.
Thoughts not yet caught up
in things to do follow the
raucous calls of crows and
wonder who they've found
to scold. A clear sense of
oneness pervades it all.
Spirit infuses the dew that
clings to every blade of
grass; Spirit lifts the front
leg of the doe as she paws
the soft ground by the salt
lick; Spirit fills me with the
buoyant certainty that this
day was made for the sole
purpose of celebrating
everything.

Small Wren Singing in the Wind

I study the way the tree limbs sway
in the wind that has huffed and galed
from the west for the last three days.

This wind spawned tornadoes in other
places, but here it comes in gusts to
lift clouds of choke cherry petals off

the trees and settle them like snow on
new spinach leaves, on lettuce, arugula
and radish tops. I study the wren,

wind ruffling the feathers of her back.
No bigger than a field mouse,
she sings with such enthusiasm,

an aria, or perhaps it is an anthem
to the wind, a folk song passed
down for more generations of

singers than she can count,
a hymn to the unpredictability
                of spring.

Mary Magdalene

Think of how it was for
her, a grieving woman
waiting through the endless,
empty Sabbath, the one she
loved, now dead.

It wasn't light yet when she
gathered up the spices and
set out, wondering aloud
how she would move the
massive rock that sealed
the tomb.

Mary Magdalene still couldn't
get her mind around the
thought that he was gone, those
fine, long fingers that could
cast out demons, or turn water
into something so intoxicating.

How could he be dead, the only
one who refused an invitation
to her bed? She could see his
sad eyes, deep as quarry
pools, offering her everything
except the one pleasure she had
longed for then.

She found the stone door
rolled aside, the gaping hole
empty, like a dark mouth waiting
to be fed. Think of that - not
even his body to anoint, no focus
for her tears.

The accounts vary here, but all
agree that something very strange
was in the wind that day. Was it
angels who told her not to
bother seeking the living among
the dead? Angels who said the
one she'd come to find was risen?

Who could believe such a message?
Surely not Mary, whose sorrow
hung about her like still air before a
storm. She was no naïve bride. No
wishful thinking would steal her
wits or numb her powers of
discernment.

But then she heard his voice.
That voice - the sound of every
question, answered. The sound
of sustenance and truth and passion.
When Mary Magdalene heard the
voice of her Beloved, she knelt in
stunned belief. "Master." It was the
only word her mouth could form.

"Peace be with you," he said.
How many times had she heard
this very greeting? But never had
it sounded like this, like music
played on harp strings by the wind.
Her pounding heart did not embrace
tranquility just then. "Do not be
afraid," he said. No, it wasn't
exactly fear she felt, but amazement.

If he could rise, then there were
no limits. Everything she

ever thought she knew was lost
in that one moment, and what
took its place could not be named,
though the pious would later call
it faith. No, what she went through
was meeting flagrant impossibility
face to face. She didn't flinch.

If he could rise, and it was
obvious he had, then there were
no rules.

She felt dizzy, giddy, light as the
chaff that rose above the pounded
grain. She went about the business
that the Master asked. She found the
disciples huddled in a room and spoke
her tale, from first to last, telling all
that she had seen and heard that
early morning, but none believed.

Think of that - the mysteries of life,
and death had been revealed to her,
and the men didn't believe a word
she said. Oh, it's not they thought
she lied - more, just, well you know
how women are, prone to exaggeration,
and seeing things, and all.

But who could believe until they'd
seen with their own eyes, heard
with their own ears, touched with
their own hands? Until Jesus
appeared to the men, Mary held the
truth in her two hands, guardian
of the flame, the one who knew

that nothing would ever be the same.

She kept her own counsel that day.
She prayed and wept and laughed
for joy, and listened to a meadowlark
as if she'd never before heard bird song.

Up In Smoke

The wind reaches cold
fingers down the stone
chimney, slips past the
flue, and whistles in
the woodstove. Oak
logs catch quickly, cast
their blazing shadows
in the dark, burn down
to glowing coals that
ignite new wood.

Everything goes up
in smoke, is snatched
by gusts and scattered
to the stars. It all burns,
ash to ash and dust to
dust. So little time for
flames to dance, so
little time.

Still Life With Vegetables

Each night I create a new
still life with vegetables.
Tonight I wonder why I
rarely cry while chopping
onions. I remember weeping
so copiously I had to grab a
napkin from its ring, but
that was years ago. Maybe
I exhaust my allotment of
tears on terrorists, use up
my crying quota listening
to stories of the newly
unemployed on NPR. I
slowly slice through a red
pepper, chop the broccoli into
flowerets, cut rounds of
carrots, just catching the one
that believed it invented
the wheel and tried rolling
off the counter. When I
finish wielding my knife
the still life that greets me,
green and orange, white and
red, arrayed on a blue plate
rescued from my grandmother's
basement after she was dead,
bears some resemblance to
Monet's garden except the
cut vegetables have sharper
edges. The carrots don't
bleed into the cilantro, and
there's no place for me to
sign my name. I consider

the Buddhist monks who
spend a month making a
perfect mandala of sand,
only to sweep it away the
day after its completion.
I think of an artist painting
over her old canvas to
start fresh – each night
a new still life. Each supper
something different to eat.

Dung Beetle

The dung beetle
walks backward,
seeing only where
he's been, never
what's in front
of him. Body
straining, he
works to maneuver
his perfect dung
ball, shaped with
precision to roll
along with him.
It's his pantry and
his pension; security
in the form of shit.
The beetle spends
his days like
Sisyphus, rolling
a known boulder
up an unseen
path to nowhere.

Hope Is Born Again

Oh, I know it's cold
outside; well below
freezing, a dry cold
that catches in the
throat. It's cold, all
right, especially when
the wind blows, but
listen to the birds.
They know that spring
is coming. Listen to
the oscillating tune of
finches, the spring trill
of a titmouse on the
feeder. Cardinals sing
as if dawn depends
upon them hitting the
high notes. The birds
haven't seen the small
green shoots poking
through the dirt. They
haven't ordered garden
seeds, or planned raised
bed plantings in their
dreams, but they know
winter is on the way out,
the cold retaining only
a temporary hold now.
The birds know that hope
is born again, long before
the promise of flowers.

Desert Dance

I danced with my Lord in
the desert and he showed
me a cactus flower, red
like the blood of a thousand
sunrises. I danced with my
Lord in the clouds, and he
presented me a garland of
shooting stars. I danced
with my Lord in the pause
between two breaths, and
he took my heart in his
hands and blessed it. We
spun for ourselves a cocoon
of silence with no beginning
and no end. We moved
until his face and mine grew
indistinct, until the whole
world turned at our fingertips,
until our essence merged and
there was only love, dancing
beyond the boundaries of
time and mind. Then love
whirled back into stillness,
back to the land of lizard and
cactus; and knew itself as One.

Two Geese

A pair of geese, silhouettes
against the steely sky, are
side by side until one goose
pulls ahead, offering a
simple gift that's instantly
accepted. The leader cuts
the air for her companion.
Now they fly single file,
just the two of them,
plaintive cries echoing
until they're out of sight.

Lazarus

It was an ordinary
day of mourning
when they followed
to the tomb.

What was he thinking,
speaking in a booming
voice, "Lazarus come
forth!" – as though life
could animate the
stinking flesh again?

You could have cut
the cynicism with a knife,
a crowd so rife with
disbelief, and yet, the authority
with which he speaks
leaves them staring.

Those with ears to hear
strained, and heard a rustle,
then the shuffle of
uncertain steps; hearts
pounding in their chests,
the very breath suspended,
the whole group took
a great step back, all
watchful in their dread.

When the dead one
appeared before them,
bound still with linen
winding sheets, no
words were spoken,

no shouts of joy, no
"welcome backs", no
congratulations to the
one who worked
this miracle.

They all dispersed, lost
in their individual musings.
If death is not death, then
what is life? The doubters
wondered if they'd been
duped. The faithful feared
their small lives
would never be the same
again. And Lazarus –
not one of them
extended him a hand.

The Rebirth
of the World

A great blue heron
flies across the red
face of the rising sun,
its crook-necked, lanky
body unmistakable.

Nature has a way of
welcoming each new
day with singular grace;
no two mornings are
the same. And I am not
a mere spectator here –

I am moved and changed,
struck dumb by loveliness,
so infused with awe and
wonder at the generosity
of mockingbirds and doves,
pine trees and high cirrus

clouds catching the first
rays of sun that I struggle
to find words. In the end
I give up and sit in silence,
cloaked in the glow of
morning, and the rebirth
              of the world.

Peggy's Cove

Lashed by wind gusts,
waves dash high against
the rocky shore. Spray
explodes skyward, salty
shrapnel stinging eyes
and cheeks. Where land
and water meet, the
ocean boils white. I sit
and let the tumult take
me where it will. I am the
bride of life, and wear a
lacy veil of sea foam in
my hair. When the wind
asks me to be true and
faithful, I dare answer
"yes," then do my best to
bend, not break, no matter
how the wind blows.

Compost Ants

The last time I dumped
our compost in the bin,

red ants swarmed with
such ferocity I swore

I'd never empty compost
there again. They poured

over the rim like miniature
Roman legions, only faster.

Perhaps, I thought, I've
wandered on the set of

some lost Hitchcock scene,
or a fifties science fiction

flick shot (badly) on a
shoestring. I couldn't

believe how aggressive
those ants were toward me.

"Disable the invader," must
be their creed, "Kill the intruder."

As they raced up my sneakers,
sinking red mandibles into my

pants, I wondered if it ever
occurred to red ants not to
bite the legs that feed them.

Weekend Forecast

The forecasters knew with
uncanny exactitude just
when yesterday's blue
sky would fill with clouds.
They issued a flood watch,
predicted the amount of
rainfall, pointed out the
wide area over which the
weekend storm would pass.

Do you think they use a
Ouija board, the whole
meteorological staff huddled
round a table, eyes following
the heart-shaped plastic
pointer beneath their fingers
spell out R – A – I – N ?

Maybe it's a crystal ball, a
man looking for all the world
like Merlin with his beard,
hired by the National Weather
Service to gaze daily, and
interpret what he sees.

Perhaps there is an expert team
of dowsers, forked sticks
pointed squarely at the sky,
or an aged woman turning
Tarot cards over one by one,
and handing her forecast to
the TV producer waiting by
the door.

I don't envy them their lot,
those meteorologists, not
even with fancy maps and
flashing radar screens.
Their job is to point out
what we humans rarely
want to see - there is
little we control, and
nothing stays the
same for very long.

Dark Angels

A pair of ravens race each
other through the yard, wings
whooshing the way I think
angels might sound. The birds
swoop in close formation into
the pine woods, flying so near
the trunks and boughs that
a collision seems almost
certain as the dark shapes
disappear in shadow. Then
I hear their guttural cries far
off in the distance, over the
lake, see them ride the west
wind high in the air and down,
a raven roller coaster without
safety belts or bars. They
make a sharp left turn and
break for the mountain, where
I've heard the thermals are
strong enough to ride all day,
if you've got the feathers for it.

Flower Seeds

When is it safe
            to sow these
flower seeds, so
            miniscule, like
grains of sand, each
            sheltering a future
burst of life and hues
            so different,
            one from the other,
like fireworks on
            the Fourth of July
waiting for the fuses
            to be lit.
The package commands,
            "Plant only when the
            danger of frost is past."
When, exactly, is that?

Who is Gardening?

Nature is the gardener on
these eight rural acres.
Sure, we pull weeds, sow
seeds, plant bulbs, move
trees, and try to keep the
riotous green of the wild
from taking over everything.
But look at the rough and
tumble wonder of the
flower garden. Columbines
and peonies crowd, cheek
to jowl as if the painter of
the canvas lost her head,
let color run rampant,
declared, "To be orderly
is tantamount to being
dead!" The poor pansies
I planted weeks ago barely
have a chance against the
unnamed undergrowth and
those sky blue blossoms
that open with the dawn
and drop their petals every
afternoon. This landscape
is too creative to be tamed,
too busy being beautiful
to be shaped, corralled or
contained. Nature's master
plan stretches far past my
small picture of a garden.

Twelve Turtles on a Log

Twelve turtles sit like tame,
round volcanoes waiting
to erupt. I try to creep up
noiselessly, but one turtle of
the dozen makes the leap to
safety (as if I'd do anything
but gaze upon smooth backs
like polished blackboards, or
marvel at the scarlet hidden
in the hollow of each
outstretched neck). When the
other turtles hear the splash
they follow in close order.
The plop of turtle shell
in lake is unmistakable.

The empty log just sits
and waits, and so do I –
unmoving, quiet. And
then one head bobs up.
Wary and alert, the turtle
stops to taste the air, swims
to the far side of the log, tries
to pull itself up – a struggle
and an unsuccessful splash.
Again, claws scratch bark,
catch, haul weight forward,
back feet flailing water, then
air, and then a balance point
is reached and passed, and
the shell tips slowly forward.

The turtle makes a quarter
turn to face the sun, and pulls

itself along the trunk until it reaches the right spot, and plants itself. This is where it makes its stand. Still life. Turtle on a log again.

The Mockingbird's Own Song

A mockingbird, invisible to me,
mimics every bird on this spacious
property. From a hidden perch,

one manic bird spins forth a flock
of chickadees, a blue jay, titmice,
crows and towhees, wrens and

finches, blackbirds, thrushes,
grackles and a dove. Does she
lose herself within the imitation?

Does she practice her own song
surreptitiously so no one else can
hear? Does she speak the secret myths

of her mockingbird lineage far into
the night when other bird songs
have grown quiet? She mimics an

indigo bunting with such skill
that I look up quickly, hoping
to see that brilliant patch of blue.

Planting Seeds

I am the ripe fruit
waiting in the tree
for the wind to rise,
or your two hands
to find me here
among the leaves.
Slowly now,
(how often have I
dreamed this moment?)
lift my round, sweet
succulence to your lips.
Taste the longing
locked within the skin,
as sun-warmed juice
drips from your chin
and forms small circles
on your shirt. A whole
life in sunlight and sap,
rainfall, bird's nests,
meteors, and the many
changing faces of the
moon. A full, rich
life led to this day's
harvest. I pray you
set aside some seeds
to plant when
the time is right.

Cape Cod Beach Walk

We walk in luminous mist,
lovers on a canvas of
sea and sand, the sound of
surf pounding. The painter
has placed us at the edge,
where land and ocean
meet, embrace, mingle and
retreat, where borders blur,
and the cadence of the waves
is like a third heartbeat
beside us.

When the tide turns and
leaves a wide expanse of
sand bar beckoning, we
wade the frigid water to
stride on the temporary
islands, marvel at the river
systems, deltas, oxbows,
braided streams racing back
to the breakers, the pull of
a distant moon leaving this
stretch of sand bare.

If we stood before this framed
painting, two figures in the fog,
edges indistinct, salt spray
hiding the details of their faces,
we'd say "I like this one," and
point at the way the couple
lean into each other, how
their posture speaks of a union
that endures despite life's
trials. We'd nod, knowing

that love is not measured in
time or miles, but by the
way the breath rises and falls
in rhythm with the waves.

Equinox

The vernal equinox ushers in the
perfect day, where neither light
nor dark predominates. Although
the sky remains the same dull and
dripping gray, I fancy there is
change – a certain brightness in
the clouds, an increase in the
calls of crows and cardinals, or
maybe it's the reflected hope
in my own eyes that adds a touch
of mystery to Spring. Several
clumps of daffodils strut their
yellow stuff as if competing for
a prize, and the worms are out in
force today, slithering across the
driveway. I step carefully around
them on my way to get the mail.
The dogwood buds – completely
closed last Sunday – are starting,
oh, so slowly, to relax their tight
grip on themselves. There is
such promise in beginnings, a
new season stretching forward
like a cat emerging from a nap,
licking long whiskers, looking
curiously around to see what
happened while it slept.

The Last Word

Take all the fear in the
world and bring it here.
Throw it in a heap. Now
find insecurity and doubt.
Locate shame and anger,
hatred and depravity.
Add them to the pile.
Find every obstacle to
love. Bring denial and
defiance, guilt, lies, and
sighs of desperation.
What does all this amount
to? How much is truth,
and how much is illusion?
If the whole world's
suffering can't asphyxiate
your love, then there is
hope for us. Hold your
love aloft in the gathering
darkness and watch peace
spread its white wings wide.
If you can keep your love
alive, then war and madness
won't have the last word.
Even now, the dove is flying.

Index of Titles and First Lines

About the Author

Danna Faulds scribbles all her poems longhand in lined notebooks, pausing during her morning yoga practice, or sitting for a few minutes after meditation. A former librarian who worked in law school, college and public libraries before turning to full-time writing, Danna lives with her husband, Richard, in the Shenandoah Valley of Virginia. Happily married for nearly 20 years, they tend an organic vegetable garden, enjoy the wildlife on their rural property, and host individuals and groups interested in the deeper practices of Kripalu Yoga.

Danna writes: *Yoga, meditation and writing have been my lifelines, allowing me to find inner connection, a greater depth of being, and a measure of serenity and joy I never imagined was possible for me. Writing helps bring those inner experiences into conscious awareness, and allows me to integrate the changes that take place as a result of my practice. Looking back, each poem played some role in my life journey.*

Having dealt with depression, self-judgment and near-paralyzing self-doubt for much of my life, I am amazed to arrive at age 50 much happier, less afraid, and more self-expressed that I ever could have imagined. It is a blessing to share this journey, and these poems, with others.

Danna can be reached by e-mail at yogapoems@aol.com